Memories

A MOTHER'S DIARY

Nelson/Regency

Memories – A Mother's Diary ©

Copyright © 1992 Sandviks Bokforlag A.S.
Illustrations © Sandviks Bokforlag in agreement with Franz Hanfstaengl.
Text and layout of original version: Eli Aleksandersen.
Text © U.S. Edition 1992 by Thomas Nelson, Inc., Nashville, Tennessee.
Family tree © Solfrid Foseide

Published in Nashville, Tennessee, by Thomas Nelson, Inc., Published and distributed in Canada by Lawson Falle, Ltd., Cambridge Ontario.

ISBN – 0840787049

Made in Belgium

2 3 4 5 6 7 8 9 10 - 96 95 94 93

To My Child

Dear _____

With all my love, I offer you this gift of memories from my own life. It is filled with my thoughts and recollections, and things that I am sure you will be happy and interested to know. When you look through this book, I hope you will remember with affection your parents and the times we spent together.

I hope also that you will enjoy having more information about your family background. Perhaps one day your own children and grandchildren will be fascinated by this record of our family's history.

Know always that the words in this book were written by a loving hand, with the intention of making the bond between us even stronger.

With love

_____

Contents

How to make the most of this book

Dear Parents,

In our lives, we play many different roles. At first, we are children ourselves, then teenagers, later partners in marriage, and parents. Each is an important part of our life story. Our part as parents comes at a stage in our lives when we are gaining immense experience. We know both the joys and the sorrows that life can bring. To our own child, we are someone who has seen a lot and who has accumulated much valuable knowledge in our journey through life.

In society today, time is a scarce commodity. To most people, a hectic working life, stress, and an apparent shortage of time are the norms. And yet, as the years pass by and we get older, time spent with our family becomes more and more precious to us - so precious that it is important to use it well now and not to waste it.

No matter how hard we try, it is not always possible for us to communicate as fully as we would wish with our children. And as the years go by there will be many things that will be forgotten. It is also often difficult to talk about thoughts and feelings. Perhaps this is because words are not the most important thing between us. Or perhaps our children are as yet too young to understand, or too young to remember what it is that we want to tell them.

But they most certainly will want to understand and know more about your life. All youngsters love stories from "the good old days" - whether they are from a grandparent's childhood, their mother's youth, or from the times when they themselves were small. Such stories and anecdotes are part of a family's history, and they are worth preserving for future generations.

How often, when we are adults, do we look back and remember the chatter and the laughter we enjoyed in the company of our parents and grandparents. We remember these occasions with warmth and affection. But over the course of years and the bustle of our own work and families, so many of these memories fade and are lost. And about the hopes and dreams of our own parents, we probably know and remember even less.

Have we ever asked them what they think of the technological innovations introduced in their lifetimes? What do they think about the political changes? Or religious developments? What is of interest to them in literature and culture? Did they participate in any of these areas of activity when they were young?

This book, **"Memories—A Mother's Diary,"** is designed to enable you to tell your story and your family's story to your child and to other members of your family. It can be used by the young mother to keep as a diary throughout her child's growing years, or by a mother who's children are now grown who wants to record and remember not only the historical facts about her life, but also her reflections, experiences, thoughts and opinions.

When you write in this book, you will give yourself a chance to think back on your life, reflect on it, and conjure up almost forgotten memories. When you have filled it in completely, you will have told the story of you and your family - a story that will be enjoyed and appreciated as a token of love. **"Memories—A Mother's Diary"** will be an important historical document that will be deeply and lastingly appreciated by the ones who are most dear to you - your family.

Within the pages of this book, we have tried to give you as much help as we can. We have given you suggestions and cues for each part of it, so that no one need wonder what to write down. There are ideas in abundance, and also plenty of extra space in which you can note additional things you may wish to include. And if you are ever really stuck for something to write, then a re-reading of this introduction will give you further inspiration and material to include.

Make a note of everything you can think of - the first time you tried to ride a bicycle, or a horse; memories of your parents, brothers and sisters; what you did at school or on holidays; information about relatives, or friends, at home or abroad; your own likes and dislikes; funny incidents, happy memories, sad memories, stories as far back as you can remember. **"Memories—A Mother's Diary"** will then be a real portrait of the family that loves and cherishes your child.

Our family tree

Grandfather

Grandmother

Father

Grandmother

Grandfather

Mother

A little about your ancestors

My mother's name is/was _____ , and she was born on

_____ in/at (place of birth) _____

Her family name was _____

She grew up in/at _____

My mother's parents were called _____

What I know about my mother's parents _____

_____

_____

_____

_____

_____

_____

_____

_____

My father's name is/was _____, *and he was born on*

_____ *in/at (place of birth)* _____

He grew up in/at _____

My father's parents were called _____

What I know about my father's parents _____

_____

_____

_____

_____

_____

_____

_____

_____

_____

_____

_____

_____

My mother and father were _____ *and* _____ *years old when they met in/at*_____

_____

They married in (year) _____ *and settled in/at* _____

_____

We were _____ *sisters and brothers, and their names are (ranked according to age):*

_____ *date of birth* _____

_____ *date of birth* _____

_____ *date of birth* _____

_____ *date of birth* _____

_____ *date of birth* _____

_____ *date of birth* _____

A little about how my mother and father met _____

_____

_____

_____

_____

_____

My Childhood

My first years

I was born in/at _____

Date of birth _____ *Weight* _____ *Height* _____

My family and friends said that I looked like _____

Now people say that I resemble _____

I was christened (full name) _____

I was so named because _____

Family/friends called me _____

I think that pet name was given to me because _____

_____

_____

When I was born, my family lived in/at _____

_____

A little about the house we lived in _____

_____

_____

_____

_____

A little about our neighbors _____

_____

_____

_____

Family and friends

The very earliest recollections I have from my childhood _____

_____

_____

_____

_____

What I remember best about my mother is this

_____

_____

_____

_____

_____

What I remember best about my father is this _____

_____

_____

_____

_____

The relationship between my sisters and brothers and myself was _____

because _____

What we did when we were together _____

_____

As a child, my best friend was called _____

Let me tell you a little about my best friend and the things we did _____

_____

_____

_____

_____

Other friends _____

_____

Pets _____

_____

My favorite things as a child

My favorite game was _____

And these were the rules of the game _____

_____

_____

My favorite toy was _____

It was given to me by _____

As a child I had a special interest for _____

My favorite sport was _____

Sports I participated in _____

_____

My favorite music and songs were _____

_____

The most popular tunes by the artist I liked best were _____

_____

My favorite book was _____ by _____

My favorite dinner was _____

and my favorite dessert _____

I also loved _____

Everyday life

I had to help out at home and my chores were to _____

_____

My father was working as _____

and my mother _____

The family economy at that time was _____

When I was _____ years old, we moved to _____

What I remember from this place _____

_____

_____

_____

_____

When I was a child, prices were completely different from today's. As far as I can remember we paid:

_____ *for a newspaper*   _____ *for a pound of coffee*

_____ *for a gallon of milk*   _____ *for a loaf of bread*

_____ *for a pound of potatoes*   _____ *for a candy bar*

_____ *for a movie*   _____ *for a stamp*

_____ *for a gallon of gas*   _____ *for a pair of shoes*

_____ *for a sports jacket*   _____ *for a football*

_____ *for a house*   _____ *for a car*

_____ *for a bus ride*   _____ *for a Christmas tree*

_____ *for a dinner at a restaurant*   _____ *for a bicycle*

An average wage was approx. _____ a year _____ a week!

A changing society

Technology was at a different stage when I was a child.
When it comes to appliances in the home, we had the
following:

_____

_____

_____

_____

As of yet we didn't have _____

_____

_____

As a child it was very fascinating to experience the following for the first time _____

_____

_____

We were also greatly impressed by new inventions like _____

_____

_____

A little about the social graces when I was a child

_____

_____

_____

_____

_____

_____

_____

_____

_____

_____

_____

_____

_____

Off to school

I started at _____ school in the year _____

I attended there for _____ years, and then I went on to _____

and _____

At that time we had a _____ hour day at school. We started at _____ o'clock and

went home at _____ o'clock in the afternoon. My favorite subjects these first years were

_____

_____

I did **not** like _____

I did well in these subjects _____

but not so well in these _____

I became friends with the following classmates _____

_____

My best friend at that time was _____

My teachers were _____

_____

_____

Special stories/memories from this period _____

_____

_____

_____

_____

_____

_____

_____

_____

_____

_____

_____

_____

_____

_____

Birthdays and holidays

This is how we celebrated Christmas when I was a child _____

_____

_____

One Christmas Day I remember especially well _____

_____

_____

_____

_____

This is how we celebrated Easter _____

_____

An Easter story from my childhood _____

_____

_____

Our family were members of _____ *Church, and our*

relationship with the church/religion was _____

_____

_____

Birthdays were celebrated like this _____

_____

_____

One birthday that stands out in my memory _____

_____

_____

We normally spent our vacations or other holidays like this _____

_____

_____

_____

_____

One vacation or holiday I remember especially well _____

_____

_____

_____

_____

_____

My dreams, expectations and memories

When I was a child, I dreamed of becoming _____

when I grew up. Other dreams I had for my future _____

_____

_____

_____

_____

What I wanted most of all was _____

_____

An especially cherished childhood memory _____

_____

_____

_____

_____

_____

_____

An especially sad memory _____

_____

_____

_____

_____

_____

_____

My youth

Fashions and trends

When I was young, fashion was different from today's. This is what my everyday clothes were like

when I was a teenager _____

_____

_____

These were my Sunday best or party clothes _____

_____

_____

My favorite clothes were _____

_____

This is the music I liked best as a teenager _____

The greatest hits were _____

_____

_____

Leisure

I liked to read the following newspapers, magazines and books _____

_____

In my spare time I preferred to _____

_____

_____

I spent the most time together with the following friends _____

_____

What we did _____

_____

On the weekends we _____

_____

My main interests were _____

_____

_____

_____

Teenager's Rebellion?

In my teens the relationship between my parents and I was _____

_____

Things we disagreed on _____

_____

_____

However, we were in full agreement when it came to _____

_____

_____

_____

My parents were strict when it came to _____

_____

but I was allowed to _____

My parents were really proud of me that time when I _____

_____

_____

And they were really annoyed with me once because I _____

_____

_____

Social Activities

I was concerned about social matters like _____

_____

Events that I got involved in _____

_____

My opinion about the government and judicial systems of those days _____

_____

_____

Future aspects that worried me _____

_____

However, I was optimistic when it came to _____

_____

As a teenager my ideals were _____

_____

because _____

_____

As a teenager I was full of principles. My most important principle was and still is _____

_____

_____

Further education

I was educated at _____

during the years _____ *to* _____ *and* _____ *to* _____

My subjects/majors were _____

_____

_____

I received certification or a degree in _____

How I liked studying _____

_____

_____

_____

A little about my life as a student _____

_____

_____

_____

I started my first job in _____. *I was working for* _____

as a _____

Other jobs I held while in school _____

_____

_____

_____

_____

Young dreams

My dreams and plans for the future _____

_____

_____

_____

_____

_____

Starting a family

I met your father _____ in the year _____

in/at (place name) _____

I was _____ years old; he was _____ . The occasion was _____

_____

My first impression of him was _____

_____

_____

Date and place of his birth _____

He has also lived in/at _____

When I met him, he lived in/at _____

_____

When we dated, we usually went to _____

_____

Sometimes we went out with other friends _____

_____

Our mutual interests _____

_____

I thought he was _____

_____

He thought I was _____

_____

Why us _____

_____

_____

_____

_____

_____

_____

_____

_____

_____

Engagement

We went together for _____ (months/years) before we got engaged. We announced our

engagement on the _____

What my parents thought of the engagement and my future husband _____

_____

What his parents thought _____

_____

It was _____ who proposed, and it happened like this _____

_____

_____

_____

Memories from the engagement period _____

_____

_____

_____

_____

_____

_____

Wedding bells ring

We got married on _____ *in* _____

church/registrar office. The ceremony was conducted by _____

and my bridesmaid(s) was/were _____

_____

and your father's best man/groomsmen was/were _____

_____

I wore a _____

and your father wore _____

The wedding was held in/at _____

The number of guests were _____

What I remember best from our wedding day is _____

_____

_____

_____

_____

_____

Our honeymoon was spent in/at _____

Memories from the honeymoon _____

_____

_____

_____

Everyday life begins

At that time we lived in a house/apartment in/at _____

What our home looked like _____

_____

_____

I was working as a _____ *and your father worked as a*

_____

My dearest memory from our first years together _____

_____

_____

_____

_____

We become parents

After _____ years together, we had our first child. We had _____ children in all, and

they are as follows:

Name   **Date of birth**

_____   _____

_____   _____

_____   _____

_____   _____

_____   _____

A little about us as parents of young children _____

_____

_____

_____

_____

_____

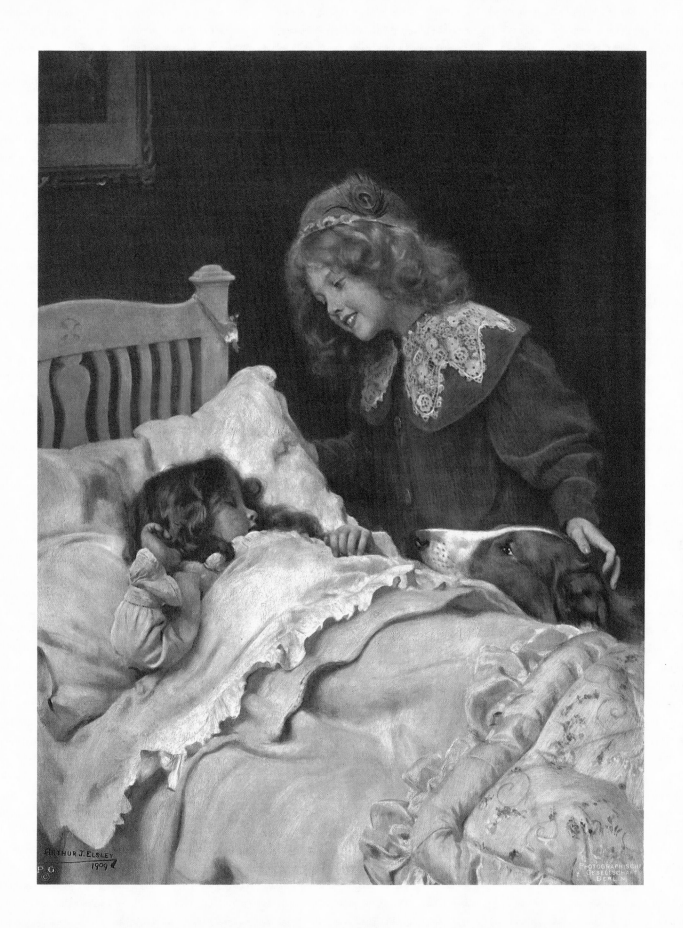

About you

You _____ *were born on* _____ *at* _____

in/at _____

At that time we lived in/at _____

We chose your name because _____

_____

We also used the pet name _____ *because* _____

_____

When you were newly born, your eyes were _____ *and your hair was* _____

My first reaction when I saw you was _____

_____

and your father's reaction was _____

_____

A little about your personality as a baby _____

_____

_____

_____

_____

Young children say the funniest things, and amusing incidents occur quite often. Here are some stories about you when you were little.

_____

_____

_____

_____

_____

_____

_____

_____

_____

_____

_____

_____

_____

_____

_____

(photo of you when you were little)   *(photo of me when I was little)*

First schools you attended _____

_____

You said your favorite subjects were _____

_____

but oh, how you disliked _____

_____

In your spare time, I could always find you _____

_____

with your little friends _____

_____

Other memories from your childhood

You reminded me of myself when you _____

_____

_____

_____

_____

You reminded me of your dad when you _____

_____

_____

_____

You were your own special person when you _____

_____

_____

_____

_____

_____

You as a teenager

You made us so proud of you when you _____

_____

_____

and we would get upset when you _____

_____

_____

In high school, I remember your worst time was _____

_____

_____

and you had the best time _____

_____

_____

The thing I will remember best about you as a teenager _____

_____

How you and I differed as teenagers _____

_____

_____

How you and I were alike as teenagers _____

_____

_____

Times change

The fashions you wore that we couldn't get used to _____

_____

Other things that were different from "my day" _____

_____

_____

(a photo of you as a teenager)   *(a photo of me as a teenager)*

Date   Age   Date   Age

Special people in our family

There are always favorite stories about favorite aunts and uncles or your sisters and brothers. Here are some I want to share with you _____

_____

_____

_____

_____

_____

_____

_____

_____

_____

_____

_____

Your paternal grandparents

About your father's parents

His mother's maiden name is/was _____ , and she was born on

_____ in/at (place of birth) _____

Her family name was _____

She grew up in/at _____

His mother's parents were called _____

What I know about these great grandparents _____

_____

_____

_____

_____

_____

_____

His father's name is/was _____ *, and he was born on*

_____ *in/at (place of birth)* _____

He grew up in/at _____

His father's parents were called _____

What I know about these great grandparents _____

_____

_____

_____

_____

_____

_____

_____

_____

_____

_____

_____

_____

_____

_____

_____

Your father's mother and father were _____ and _____ years old when they met in/at

_____

They married in (year) _____ and settled in/at_____

_____

Your father was number _____ of _____ sisters and brothers, and their names are

(ranked according to age):

_____ *date of birth* _____

_____ *date of birth* _____

_____ *date of birth* _____

_____ *date of birth* _____

_____ *date of birth* _____

_____ *date of birth* _____

A little about how his mother and father met _____

_____

_____

_____

_____

_____

About you and your grandparents

Waiting for you

The news that you were on the way was presented to both sets of grandparents like this

_____

_____

_____

_____

_____

These were their reactions _____

_____

_____

_____

_____

When you were very little you called your grandparents _____

_____

Sometimes we let you stay with your grandparents. These are some of the special times you had

with them (maternal and paternal) _____

_____

_____

_____

_____

_____

_____

_____

They used to call you pet names _____

_____

These are some of the special things they said about you _____

_____

_____

_____

Family traditions

This is how our family celebrated Christmas when you were a child _____

_____

_____

_____

_____

_____

On Christmas Day we ate _____

but you had special likes and dislikes _____

_____

Easter was usually celebrated like this _____

_____

My favorite Easter story about you _____

_____

_____

Other regular family gatherings _____

_____

_____

_____

_____

"Secret" family recipes
(Note down the recipes for your family's specialties or the food your child most likes for you to fix.)

_____

_____

_____

_____

_____

_____

_____

_____

_____

_____

_____

_____

_____

_____

_____

_____

Other family traditions

Every family has its traditions. Here are some of ours _____

_____

_____

_____

_____

_____

Leisure and travels

When the children were young, we usually spent our vacations or holidays at/in _____

_____

_____

_____

As the children grew up, these are some of the special travels or vacations we had _____

_____

_____

_____

_____

Some of us liked traveling; some of us didn't _____

_____

_____

Our first experience with traveling abroad _____

_____

I have done some traveling by myself or with your father _____

_____

_____

_____

_____

The most beautiful place I ever spent my vacation or holidays in is _____

_____

_____

_____

I was there in _____ *with* _____

Things I learned by experience on my travels _____

_____

_____

_____

_____

Our best vacation/trip as a family _____

_____

_____

_____

Holiday memories

My working life

I started my career as _____

That was in 19 _____ *I was* _____ *years old, and I was working for* _____

_____

The most important stages in my education and career _____

_____

_____

_____

_____

I spent most of my working life as a _____

_____

_____

The most important experiences gained during my working life were _____

_____

_____

_____

_____

_____

_____

_____

What my work has meant to me _____

_____

_____

_____

_____

_____

_____

_____

_____

_____

_____

The best piece of advice I can give you when it comes to choosing a career is this _____

_____

_____

_____

Happy memories from where/when I worked _____

_____

_____

_____

_____

_____

_____

My interests

One of my greatest interests over the years has been _____

_____

_____

Why I enjoyed this activity _____

_____

_____

_____

_____

Other activities, sports and social matters I have participated in _____

_____

_____

_____

_____

My favorite books _____

_____

_____

_____

My favorite music _____

_____

_____

Other favorites (e.g. actors, plays, films, television programs, magazines, periodicals, etc.)

_____

_____

_____

_____

People I admire _____

_____

_____

_____

My philosophy of life - what gives my life meaning

_____

_____

_____

_____

_____

_____

_____

_____

_____

_____

_____

_____

_____

Society then and now

I feel the following to be the most important discoveries and inventions in my time...

_____

_____

_____

_____

_____

_____

_____

_____

_____

_____

_____

The most important political events in our country during this period _____

_____

_____

_____

_____

The most important international events have been _____

_____

_____

_____

_____

To me personally, the most important changes

socially/politically have been _____

_____

_____

_____

_____

_____

The most positive social changes in our time have been _____

_____

_____

_____

The most negative _____

_____

_____

_____

What I miss most and least from "the good old days" _____

_____

_____

_____

_____

_____

_____

What the future may hold

What I think the world will be like when you are my age

_____

_____

_____

_____

_____

My wishes for your future, my dear child

_____

_____

_____

_____

_____

I forgot to tell you about

Other things I remember now that you may like to know or may find useful

Memories and photos

Here are some photographs, newspaper clippings and other mementoes for you. (Photos, tickets, a lock of hair, newspaper announcements of births, engagements and weddings, etc.)

Thoughts and reflections

Now I will let my mind wander freely and write a little about what has meant most to me in my life. My thoughts, reflections, attitudes, principles, sorrows and joys...